MARIN MARAIS

(1656-1728)

FIVE OLD FRENCH DANCES

FOR VIOLA (OR VIOLIN OR VIOLONCELLO)

WITH PIANOFORTE ACCOMPANIMENT

ARRANGED BY MAUD E. ALDIS AND LOUIS T. ROWE.
(THE VIOLONCELLO PART BY MAY MUKLE.)

CINQ DANSES FRANÇAISES ANCIENNES

POUR ALTO (OU VIOLON OU VIOLONCELLE)

AVEC PIANO

ARRANGÉES PAR MAUD E. ALDIS ET LOUIS T. ROWE.
(LA PARTIE DE VIOLONCELLE PAR MAY MUKLE.)

CHESTER MUSIC

In order to provide a suitable version for cello, the third movement 'La Musette' has been transposed down a fourth to G minor. This appears on alternate pages 7a and 8a, after the original version in C minor for violin or viola.

I.
L'AGRÉABLE.
RONDEAU.

M. Marais.

Moderato.

Viola (Alto)
Violin or Violoncello.

PIANO.

II.
LA PROVENÇALE.

III.
LA MUSETTE.

Tempo primo.

Marin Marais
FIVE OLD FRENCH DANCES

CHESTER MUSIC

VIOLONCELLO.

I.
L'AGRÉABLE.
RONDEAU.

M. Marais.

VIOLONCELLO.

II.
LA PROVENÇALE.

VIOLONCELLO.

III.
LA MUSETTE.

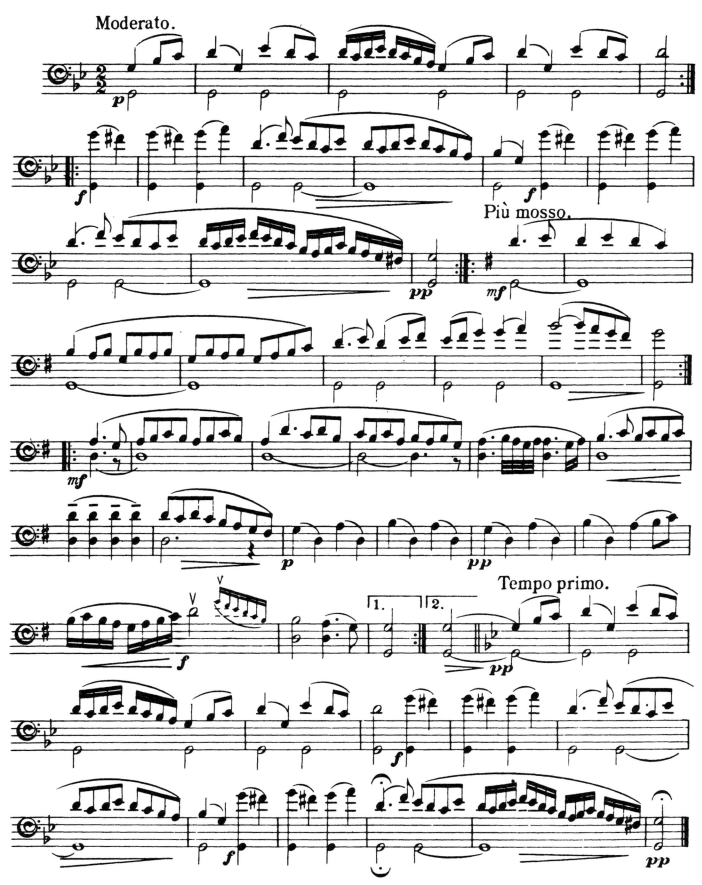

An alternative piano part is required for this movement, as it has been transposed down a fourth to suit the cello.

VIOLONCELLO.

IV.
LA MATELOTTE.

Gaiement.

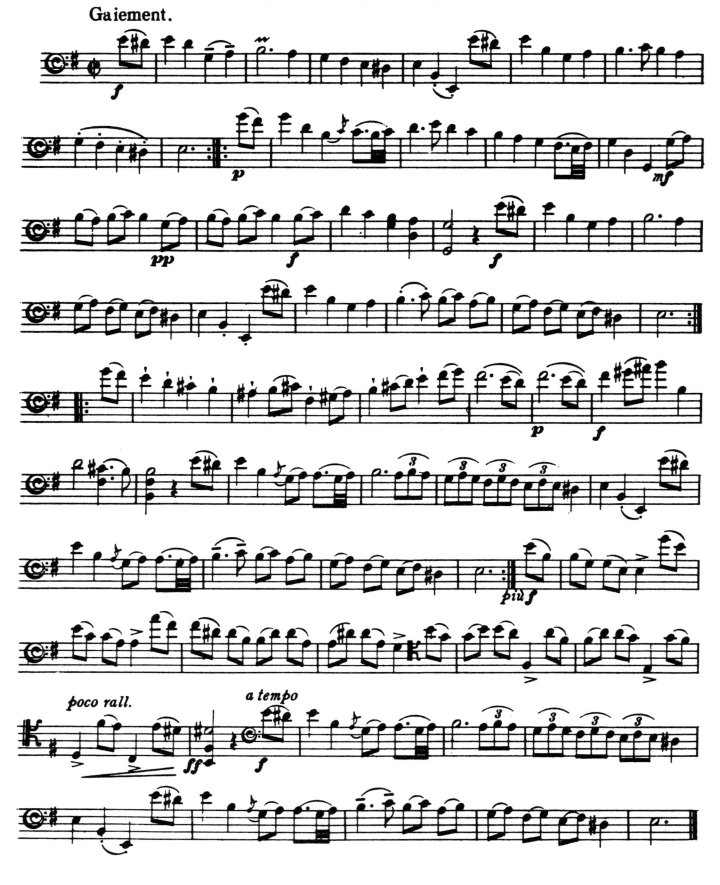

VIOLONCELLO.

V.
LE BASQUE.

Marin Marais
FIVE OLD FRENCH DANCES

CHESTER MUSIC

I.
L'AGRÉABLE.
RONDEAU.

M. Marais

Moderato.

p IIª volta 8va ad lib.

cresc.

p

mf

p

cresc.

f

poco rall.

II.
LA PROVENÇALE.

III.
LA MUSETTE.

IV.
LA MATELOTTE.

V.
LE BASQUE.

Marin Marais
FIVE OLD FRENCH DANCES

CHESTER MUSIC

I.
L'AGRÉABLE.
RONDEAU.

M. Marais.

© Copyright, 1990 for all Countries
Chester Music Ltd. 8/9 Frith Street, London W1V 5TZ   CH5636

VIOLA.(Alto)

II.
LA PROVENÇALE.

VIOLA.(Alto)

III.
LA MUSETTE.

VIOLA.(Alto)

IV.
LA MATELOTTE.

Gaiement.

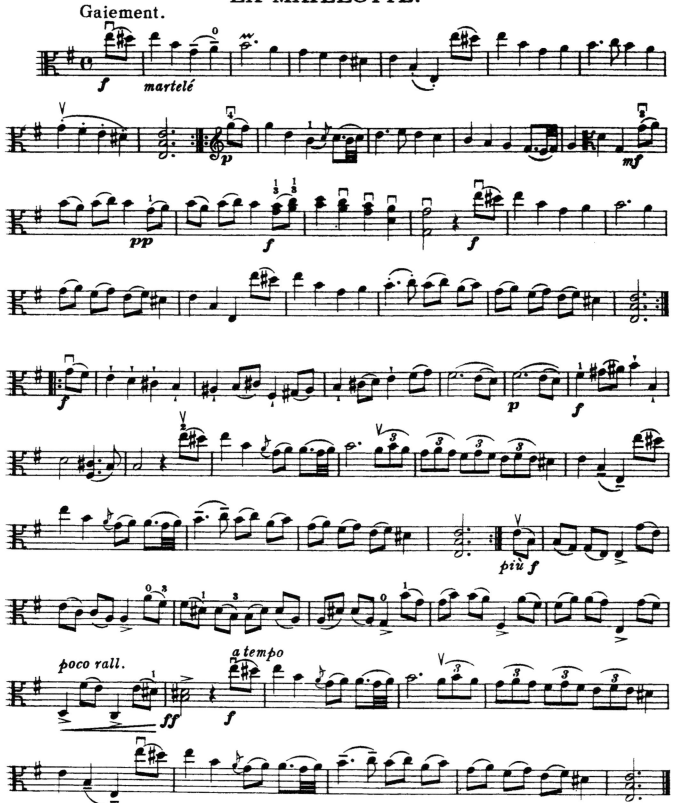

VIOLA. (Alto)

V.
LE BASQUE.

III.
LA MUSETTE.

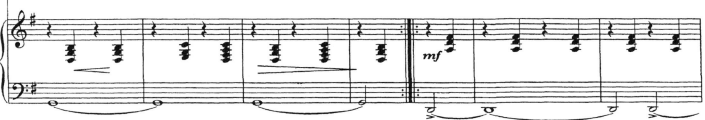

Tempo primo

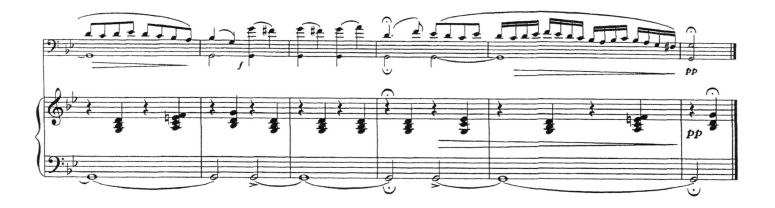

IV.
LA MATELOTTE.

V.
LE BASQUE.

Vivace.

Double.

PLAYSTRINGS

MUSIC FOR
STRING ORCHESTRA

MUSIQUE POUR
ORCHESTRE A CORDES

MUSIK FÜR
STREICHORCHESTER

MÚSICA PARA
INSTRUMENTOS
DE ARCO

弦楽オーケストラ作品

EASY /Facile /Sehr Leicht /Facil /「易しい」

E.1 **THREE PIECES BY DIABELLI** arr. Anita Hewitt-Jones

E.2 **THREE TUNES FROM SHAKESPEARE'S ENGLAND**
arr. Nicholas Hare
Go from My Window; Greensleeves; Nobodyes Gigge

E.3 **THE CIRCUS COMES TO TOWN** Jill Townsend
*A colourful evocation of the excitement of the saw-dust ring,
portraying the Ringmaster, Lions, Elephants, Tight-rope Walkers, etc.*

E.4 **FUN AND GAMES** Jill Townsend
A lively sequence of traditional children's games

E.5 **WHIRLIGIG** Anita Hewitt-Jones
Waltz; Windmills; Ragtime

E.6 **PURCELL IN MINIATURE** arr. Watson Forbes
Trumpet Tune; Minuet; Ayre; Scotch Tune; Irish Tune; Riggadoon

E.7 **SPACE TRAVELLERS** Bruce Lawrence
*In Orbit; March of the Androids; In Deep Space;
Lords of the Galaxy*

E.8 **STRAWBERRY FAIR** Sally Knight
*Strawberry Fair; Dame get up and Bake your Pies;
The Keeper*

E.9 **LAND OF HOPE AND GLORY** arr. Stuart Barrie
Themes from Pomp and Circumstance

E.10 **SOUNDS FROM SCOTLAND** arr. Stuart Barrie
Lewis Bridal Song; Skye Boat Song; Loch Lomond

MODERATELY EASY /Moyenne Force /Leicht /Mediana Dificultad /「やや易しい」

M.E.1 **A SUITE OF ENGLISH FOLKSONGS** arr. Rory Boyle

M.E.2 **DANCE SUITE** Jill Townsend

M.E.3 **CZECH SONG AND DANCE** Jill Townsend

M.E.4 **FRIDAYS, SATURDAYS** Jill Townsend

M.E.5 **THE PIRATES OF PENZANCE** Sullivan

M.E.6 **MOZART IN MINIATURE** arr. Watson Forbes

M.E.7 **THE WHITE KNIGHT AND THE DRAGON** John Cameron

M.E.8 **PRELUDE AND FUGUE FOR FUN** Anthony Hedges

M.E.9 **HANDEL IN MINIATURE** arr. Watson Forbes

M.E.10 **RUSTIC DANCES** Christopher Brown

*Scores, issued separately, and sets of parts
are available from*

CHESTER MUSIC